The Galactic Gallery

BAARGAVI S

Dedicated to Lucky and Cwaso, the sweetest and cutest little cockatiels I have ever known.

Acknowledgments

I sincerely thank my parents for their immeasurable support throughout my journey of writing this book. I would also like to thank my best friend Madeeha for all her support and help. She helped me in many ways and also helped me design the cover of this book.

Welcome to the Galactic Gallery

Meet your guides

Dear Visitor, you will have two guides, Lucky and Cwaso, who will be showing you around the gallery and illustrating the message that each of the paintings are trying to convey to you.

Name : Lucky
Age : 4 Years
Type : Pearl Cockatiel
Favorite Color : Purple
Favorite Food : Paddy Seed

Name : Cwaso
Age : 2 Years
Type : Pied Cockatiel
Favorite Color : Pink
Favorite Food : Sunflower Seed

Dear Visitor, me and cwaso own this gallery. Let me tell you about it. In this gallery, we have themed exhibitions every year, where people submit their artwork anonymously and explain the message they convey to us, which we then convey to our visitors.

This year's theme is the Universe, with a focus on the formation of the universe. We've got many submissions so far. Let us show them to you. First, let us look further into our theme- the universe.

The Universe

The universe is all of space and all of time. It comprises all of existence, and all forms of matter & energy, and the structures they form, from sub-atomic particles to entire galaxies. Before the universe came into existence, there was absolutely nothing, no matter, no energy, no space and no time. The universe is 13.8 billion years old.

The Big Bang

This painting represents the big bang. Let me tell you about it. At one point, the entire universe was a tiny dot, so small it couldn't be seen by the naked eye. This dot was infinitely hot and dense. This dot exploded and started expanding on an exponential scale. This was the start of it all, all the space, time, matter and energy in the universe. As this dot started expanding into the universe, it cooled down as well. At these early times, all the fundamental forces were unified into a single force, before separating a little later. Cwaso will explain these forces to you, dear visitor.

Fundamental Forces

This painting represents the fundamental forces. The fundamental forces are the forces which govern all interactions between particles in the universe. These include:

The **strong nuclear force** is the strongest of the four forces and works in the nucleus of atoms. It holds the nucleus together by counteracting the repulsion of protons in the nucleus. But this force has a really small range.

The **weak nuclear force** is a million times weaker than the strong nuclear force and has an even smaller range. It is responsible for things like beta decay of particles, where neutrons turn into protons, releasing high energy electrons or positrons (the antimatter equivalent of an electron).

The **electromagnetic force** is the second strongest force and has infinite range. It is responsible for the attraction and repulsion between charged objects and also for the creation of magnetic fields. It controls how electrons behave.

The **gravitational force** is the weakest of the 4 forces, but is still strong enough to hold stars and galaxies together.

All these forces are explained by the **standard model**, which is a remarkable insight into the structure of matter, stating that everything in the universe is made up of a few basic particles called fundamental particles, governed by four fundamental forces. This theory encapsulates how these particles and three of the forces are related to each other.

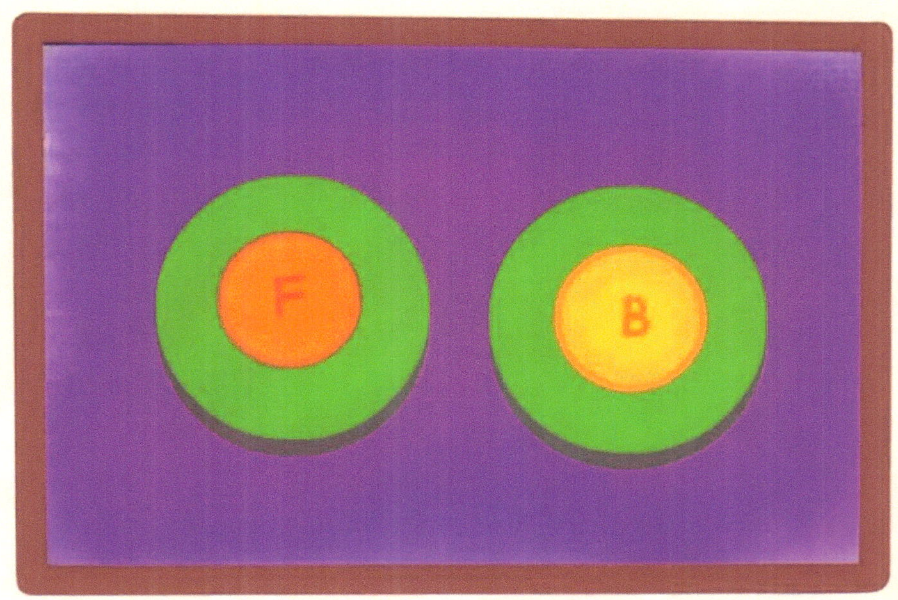

Fundamental Particles

This painting represents the fundamental particles. The fundamental particles are the basic particles that make up the universe. They are divided into matter particles (fermions) and force carrier particles (bosons).

Fermions make up all the matter in the universe. They are divided into quarks and leptons. These quarks and leptons are further divided into three generations, which are divisions in which the particle's interactions are identical, but the particles are more massive.

Bosons are the force carriers within the fundamental forces, which exchange these forces between particles. Each fundamental force has its own corresponding boson: The strong nuclear force is carried by the gluon, the electromagnetic force is carried by the photon, and the weak nuclear force is carried by the W and Z bosons. There is also a theoretical graviton, which is supposed to carry the gravitational force, but it hasn't been discovered yet.

The very Early Universe

This painting represents the very early Universe. Let me tell you about it. The universe was much hotter, denser and energetic in the past. During these times, all the four fundamental forces were unified into one.
Gravity is thought to have separated first, followed by the strong nuclear force from the electroweak force. As the universe cooled and expanded, the electroweak force separated into the electromagnetic and weak nuclear forces.

Formation of Matter &
Antimatter

Dear visitor, this painting represents the creation of matter and antimatter in the universe. Let me tell you about it. The first particles were created within the first microseconds of the universe. However, the creation of these particles had a limit — these particles could only be created in pairs, particle and antiparticle. Usually, these pairs collided and annihilated immediately and their energy was carried away by photons. However, as the universe underwent inflation, these pairs that would annihilate almost immediately got separated, leading to a flood of matter and antimatter.

In this inflated universe, these particles and antiparticles annihilated again, releasing a wave of gamma rays, that could collide and create pairs again. For a brief period of time, annihilation and pair production were balanced. But as the universe expanded, it reduced the temperature of the particles, which lead to a period called quark confinement. Before this, the universe had too much energy for groups of quarks to settle into combinations of quarks, like protons and neutrons. Quark confinement allowed the formation of these protons and neutrons.

For some unknown reason, matter outnumbered antimatter by about 1 billion to 1. A wave of annihilation occurred, and this 1 part in a billion formed the observable universe. As the universe cooled further, no more protons, neutrons or their antiparticles could be created. At 1 second old, it cooled down enough for electrons and positrons to survive. So, at 1 second old, the universe had many protons, neutrons, electrons and high energy photons.

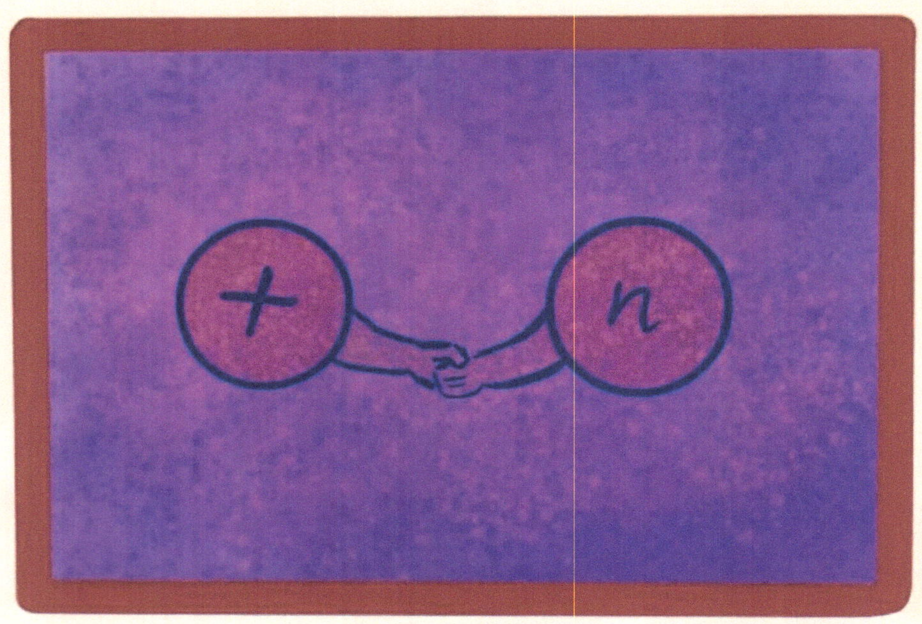

Nucleosynthesis

This painting represents big bang nucleosynthesis. Let me tell you about it. As the Universe cooled further, it created conditions suitable for protons and neutrons to join and form the first atomic nuclei. It is said to have created light nuclei like deuterium, helium and Lithium. It occurred with in 10 seconds and 20 minutes after the Big Bang.

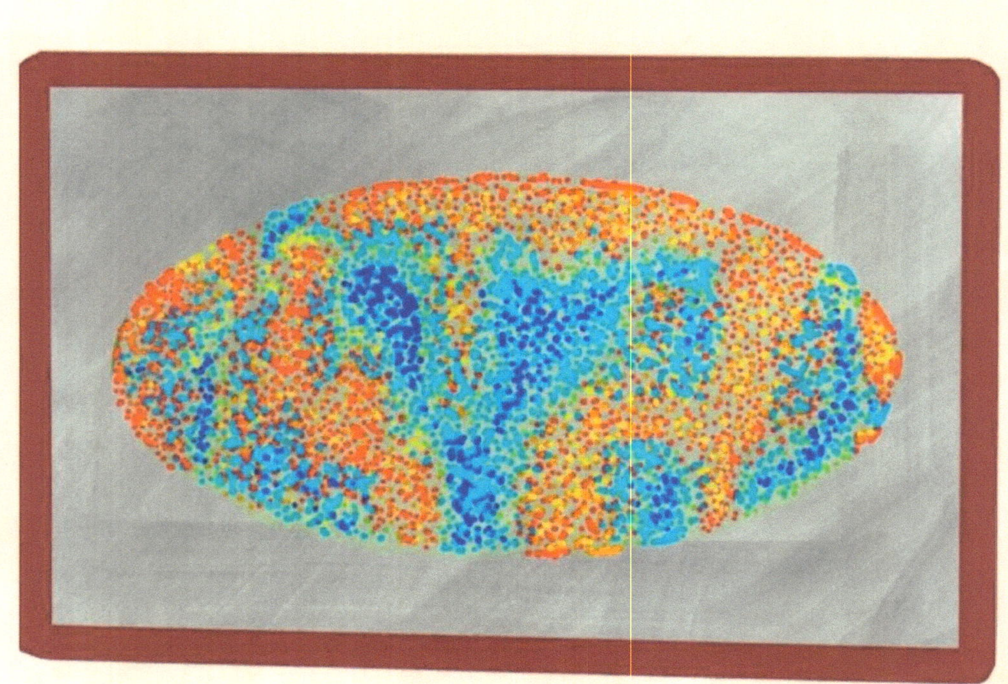

Recombination

This painting represents **recombination**. Let me tell you about it. Before recombination, the universe was so hot and particles were moving so fast that every time an electron and proton came together, they were knocked apart by photons. So, the universe was an ionised plasma with atomic nuclei, electrons and photons.
When it was 380,000 years old, its temperature reduced enough for photons to lose enough energy to not be able to knock electrons out of their orbits around protons. So, protons could finally capture electrons and become complete atoms. This is called Recombination. It formed neutral Hydrogen atoms.

Because of recombination, electrons no longer got in the way of photons, allowing them to travel freely as radiation throughout the early Universe. This was called as photon de-coupling.
This radiation can be seen as the cosmic microwave background in examined signals.
The cosmic microwave background also helped prove the big bang theory.

Cosmic Dark Age

This painting represents the **cosmic dark ages.** During the cosmic dark ages, the universe was full of neutral hydrogen atoms and lacked stars and galaxies, so there was no light.
Also, matter was distributed fairly evenly across the universe. However, the universe was not completely homogenous, as there were density fluctuations in the hydrogen gas in the universe, which then formed the first stars.

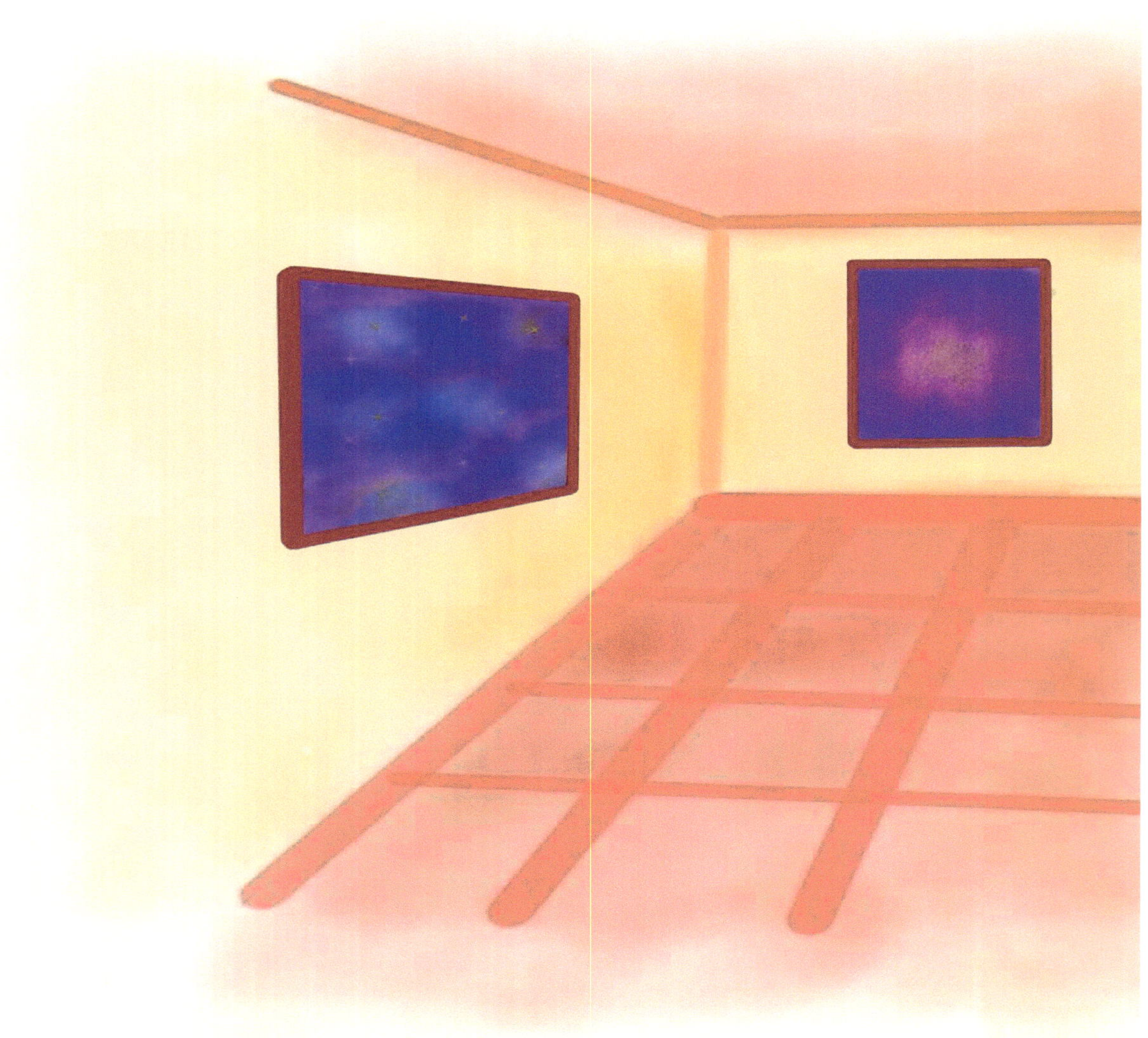

First Stars

This painting represents the **first stars.** I'll tell you about it. There were some regions in the universe with a higher density of matter than others. The gravity of these regions attracted more and more matter towards them. Eventually, these clumps of matter reached sufficient densities and temperatures to ignite fusion reactions, forming the first stars called Population III stars.

The formation of these stars produced many high-energy photons which could strip electrons from protons, in a process called ionization.
They were mostly made of hydrogen and helium and had a very low metallicity (the amount of elements other than hydrogen and helium they contain). They were very massive and hot, which led to them having short lifespans.

Death of First Stars

This painting portrays the **Death of first stars**. I'll tell you about it.
In these stars, nuclear fusion produced huge amounts of energy which pushed outwards. At the same, gravity pushed inwards. So, both these forces were balanced.
But as these stars ran out of hydrogen, they started fusing heavier elements like Helium, producing elements like Carbon, Oxygen and eventually Iron. Iron didn't fuse with other elements, ending nuclear fusion. As these stars fused heavier elements, they swelled up to a huge size.

After fusion, these stars died in explosions called Supernovae. As there isn't any fusion left to push outwards, the star collapses in on itself because of gravity. It then rebounds violently, and blows away its outer layers with great force.
These supernovae dispersed heavy elements throughout the universe, helping in the formation of nebulae and population II stars.

First Nebulae

This painting represents the First Nebulae. Let me tell you about it.

These scattered elements from supernovae mixed with the Hydrogen and Helium already in space, forming giant molecular clouds of gas and dust. These are called nebulae.

These nebulae were pretty stable, until they were disturbed in some way, such as a passing star or super nova. When this happens, parts of nebula collapsed into denser clumps with increasing gravity, pulling in more and more material.

The clump's center grew hotter and denser until it became a star.
But these stars were different, they were much smaller and had a much higher metallicity. They were called population II stars.
Thus, these nebulae were breeding grounds for population II stars.

You will need to know about a few things before learning about the next two paintings. First you would need to know about inertia. What is Inertia?

Inertia is the property of an object that allows it to stay at rest or in uniform motion in a straight line, unless it's acted upon by an external force. So, an inertial frame of reference/inertial observer is one that is either at rest or moving with a constant speed in a straight line. Inertial observers are weightless.

Next, you would need to know about a photon clock. What is a photon clock?

A photon clock consists of two mirrors and a photon bouncing between them. It's said that one bounce of the photon between the mirrors signifies one unit of time.

Special Theory of Relativity

Now, let us talk about the next two paintings. this painting represents Einstein's **special theory of relativity.** let me tell you about it. Einstein's special theory of relativity is based on 2 postulates.

- The laws of physics are the same for all observers in inertial frames of reference. So, whether you are at rest or in uniform motion (moving at constant speed), the laws of physics will be the same for you.
- The speed of light in a vacuum is constant. It will always be 3×10^8 m/s

Let us discuss a few key concepts in Special relativity. let's start with Time dilation.

Time dilation basically states that time passes slower when you move at really high speeds. Let us see how it works with an example.
So, imagine a photon clock on a spaceship. If the spaceship is at rest, the photon moves up and down from point A to B within the walls of the photon clock.

Now imagine this spaceship starts moving at a very high speed. The photon clock itself also starts moving along with the photon. So, the points A and B on the photon clock also move. When A & B were at rest, the photon moved up and down between them. But when they start moving, the photon would have to catch up to these moving points, increasing the distance it covers because it now moves on a slanted path. Thus the number of times the photon will bounce off the mirror, or the number of units of time will be reduced. So, time will move slower.

Let me talk about length contraction now. Length contraction states that for a moving object, the length of the path it covers along with that of objects on the way appears to be smaller than it does to an observer at rest. Time dilation and length contraction go hand-in-hand and we can understand this using the formulas of speed, distance and time.

$$\text{Speed} = \frac{\text{Distance}}{\text{Time}} \quad \text{and distance} = \text{speed x time}$$

so, l = constant speed of light x dilated time
Therefore, this would result in smaller or contracted length

In the Special theory of relativity Einstein talked about **Energy-Mass equivalence /** $E=mc^2$ as well. Let me explain:
It states that mass can be converted into energy and vice versa. This is because energy is required to create the forces which bind the particles that make up the atoms of this matter and thus its mass.

General Theory of Relativity

This painting represents Einstein's **General Theory of relativity**. let me tell you about it. The general theory of relativity states that gravity is not a force, but a combination of curvature of spacetime as well as acceleration (which gives us weight). Let me explain:

Imagine a spaceship in inertial motion and there is a planet nearby. The spaceship will move closer to the planet and crash into it. But why? You might think that this would happen because there is a gravitational force attracting the spaceship towards the planet

But according to general relativity, this is not the case. Einstein said that the spaceship's trajectory was curved because the planet had warped the space around it. This space that the planet warped is called Spacetime. what is spacetime? Einstein said that space and time aren't separate. Time is also another physical dimension and together the three dimensions of space (length, breadth, height), along with one dimension of time combine to form a four-dimensional geometry called spacetime. Any mass, like a planet can warp or curve this spacetime.
Thus, spacetime can be defined as a four-dimensional geometry formed by the physical dimensions of space and time, which can be warped by a mass.

Let's go back to our example. The spaceship was moving in a straight line. But the spacetime around the planet was curved by its mass. So, the spaceship was moving in a straight line in curved spacetime. This is a geodesic.

Now imagine you're in this spaceship and you turn on the blasters and start accelerating at exactly $9.8 \, m/s^2$. Someone outside your spaceship would see you and other objects inside the spaceship as staying still while the bottom of the spaceship accelerates towards you.

Inside, you would feel like you are accelerating downwards and there is a force pushing on you. This feels exactly like being on earth. This is because it is the exact same thing. You, me and everything on earth is accelerating.

Let me show you: According to Newton's 3rd law of motion, every action has an equal and opposite reaction. So according to Newton, there is a gravitational force pushing downwards and an opposite force pushing upwards. But Einstein says there is no gravitational force, so only the opposite force remains. This opposite force is termed as acceleration.

But if earth's surface is expanding, wouldn't the earth expand? well not really. Einstein's general theory of relativity contains an equation which basically states that your change in position would be equal to your acceleration minus the curvature of spacetime. So, your change in position can be zero. But for that to happen, your acceleration must match the curvature of spacetime.

The general theory of relativity has many effects. One of these effects is **gravitational time dilation**. Let me explain:

Einstein also said that you would experience time dilation when you're around a massive object, like a black hole.

Let's use a photon clock to understand this concept. If a photon clock is exposed to a mass, like a black hole, the photon inside will be slowed by the curvature of spacetime. This is because time is affected by the curvature of spacetime. Thus, the number of times the photon will bounce off the mirror, or the number of units of time will be reduced. So, time will move slower.

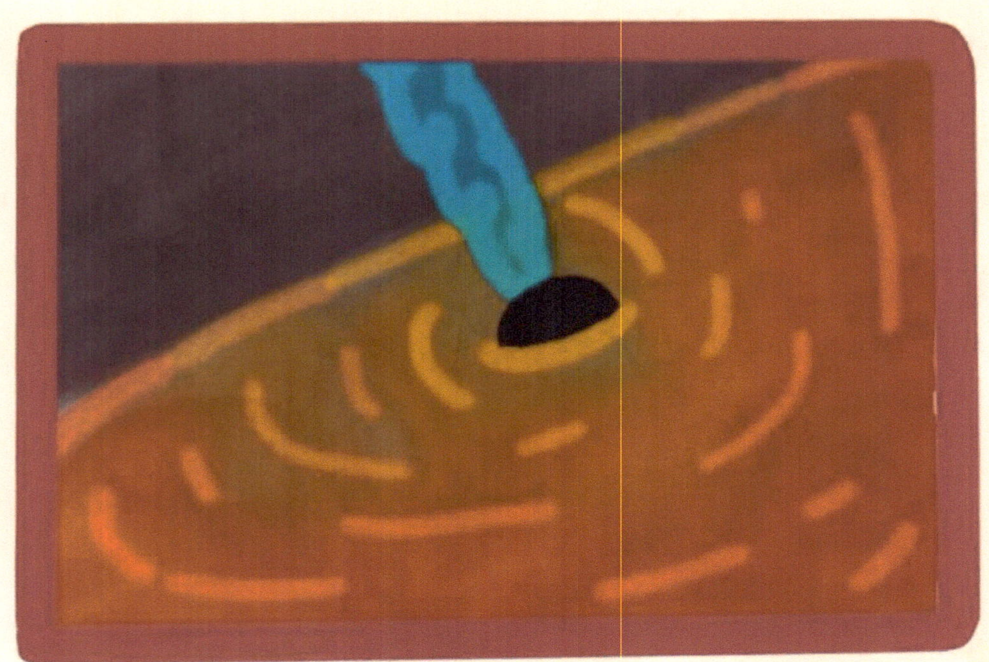

First Black Holes

This painting represents the first black holes.
Let me tell you about it.
After going supernova, these population III
stars also left behind a dense core, which
collapsed into a black hole. This is how stellar-
mass black holes were formed.
Supermassive black holes may have been formed
by two smaller black holes colliding or even by
large gas clouds directly collapsing into black
holes.

These black holes warp spacetime in such a way that matter and energy cannot escape them. So, anything that passes into this sphere (called the event horizon) is lost to the universe. This warping of spacetime is also so severe that it results in a **singularity** - an extremely dense point in space with no volume.

First Galaxies

This painting represents the first galaxies. Let me tell you about it.
Galaxies are collections of stars, nebulae and other matter held together by gravity. The first stars were formed in small groups. These small groups clustered together due to gravity, forming the first galaxies.
However, these galaxies were much smaller than the ones we see today and were also irregularly shaped.

The larger, more stable galaxies we see today could have been formed by mergers between these smaller galaxies.
Dark matter (an invisible type of matter that only interacts with regular matter through gravity) clumped together, creating an area with more gravity which attracted regular matter towards it, helping form these galaxies.

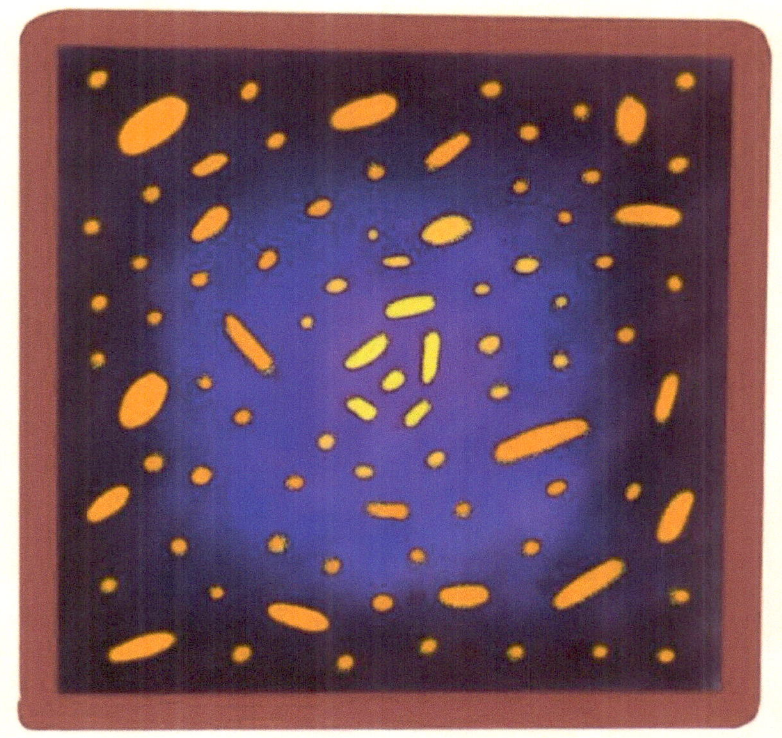

Galaxy Clusters and Super Clusters

This painting represents the galaxy clusters and super clusters. Let me tell you about it.
Galaxy clusters are large groups of galaxies bound together by gravity. They were formed by dark matter clumping together and forming gravitational wells, around which galaxies gathered.
Galaxy super-clusters are even larger. They are groups of galaxy clusters formed by the gravitational pull between them.

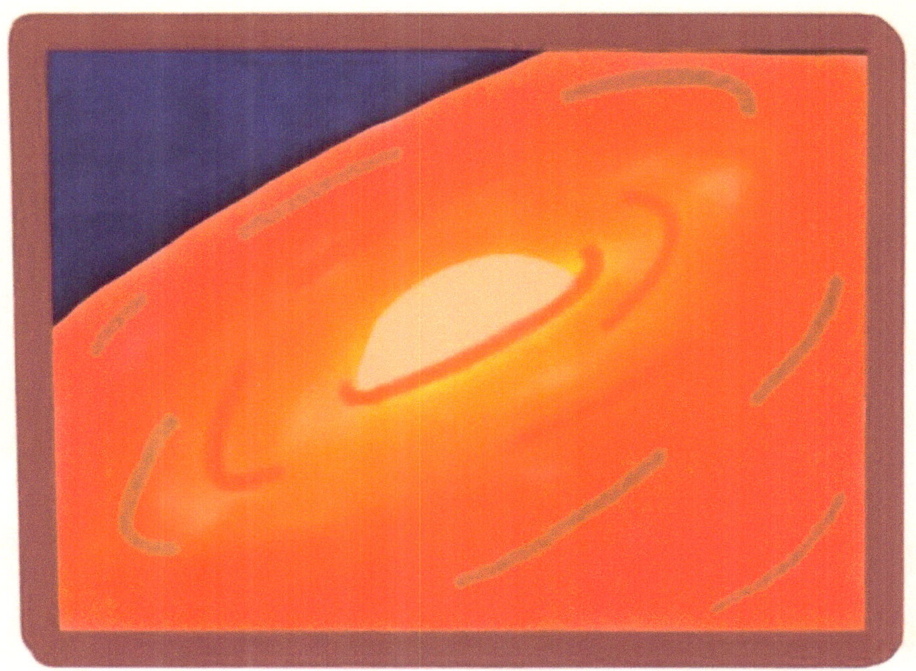

Formation of Solar System

This painting represents the formation of the Solar System. Let me explain:
The solar system was formed 4.6 billion years ago from a giant cloud of gas and dust which collapsed under its own gravity, forming a spinning disk called the solar nebula. This collapse may have been triggered by a shockwave from a nearby supernova.
More material was pulled to the center of this nebula by gravity, eventually forming the Sun.

The rest of the matter started clumping together. These clumps crashed into each other, forming bigger ones. Some of them grew big enough for their gravity to shape them into spheres; forming planets, dwarf planets and some big moons. The rest became asteroids, comets meteorites and small irregular moons.

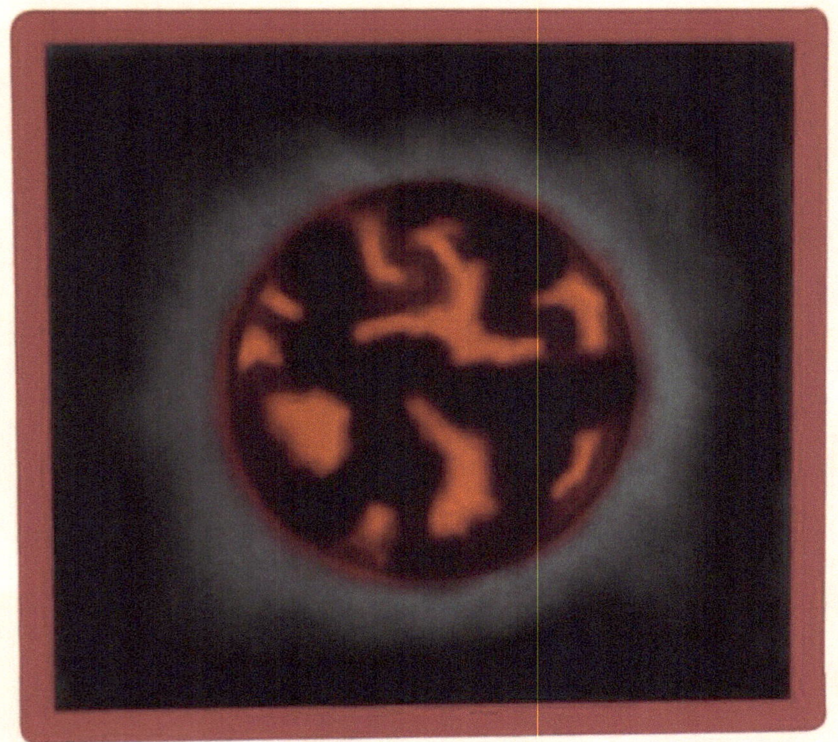

Formation of the Earth

This painting represents the **formation of the Earth**. Let me explain:

As the clumps of matter around the Sun collided with each other, they formed larger objects called planetestimals. They collided further, forming larger bodies. One of these was Earth. During this time, it was very hot and the material inside started to melt, forming layers. A collision with a Mars-sized object sent debris flying into space, which then came together due to gravity and formed the Moon.

Eventually, the Earth cooled down enough to harden, forming the crust. Volcanic activity released water vapour, carbon dioxide and nitrogen, which formed the atmosphere. Water collected on the surface, forming the oceans.

Welcome to the galactic
gift shop

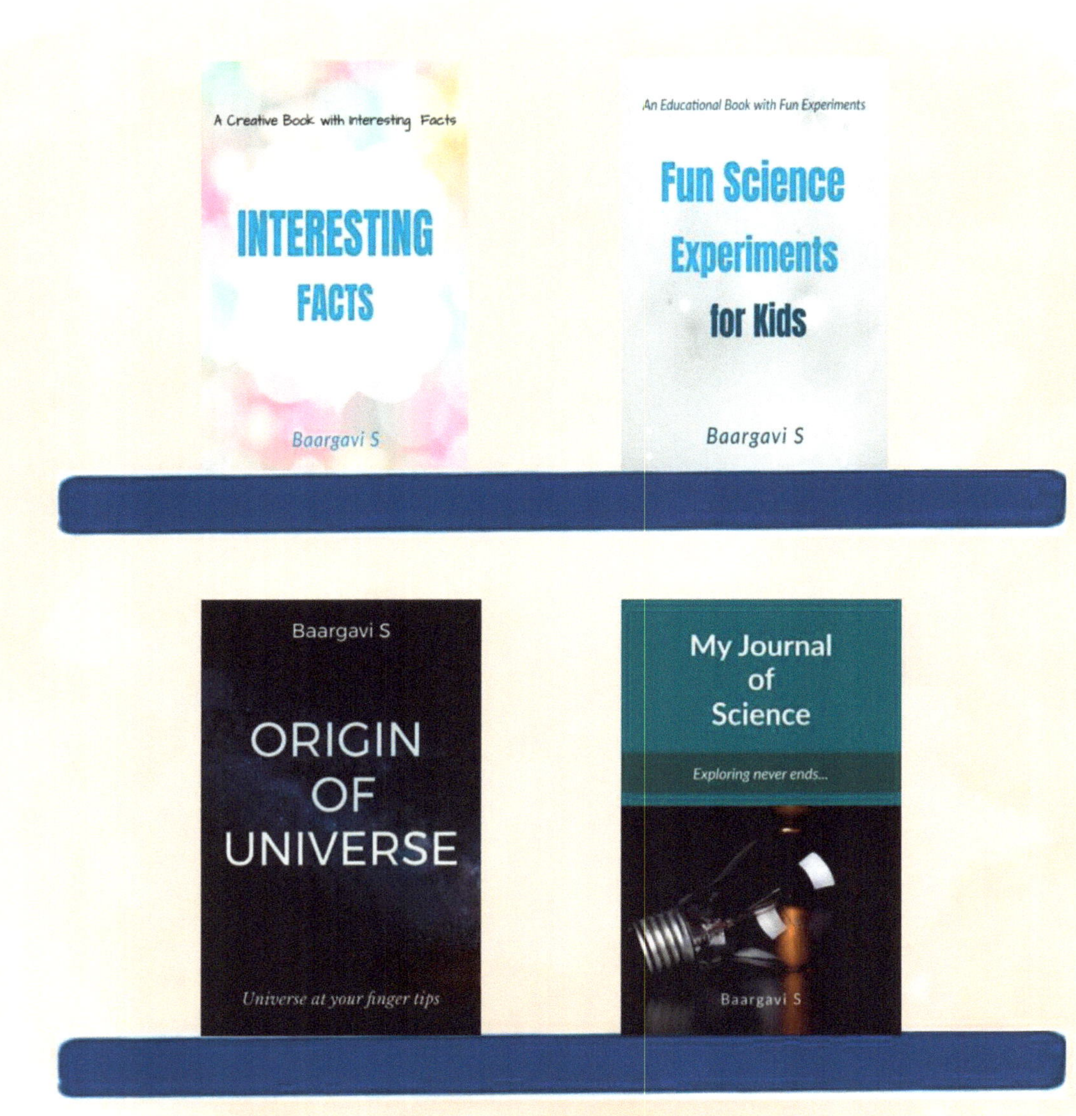
A Creative Book with Interesting Facts
INTERESTING
FACTS
Baargavi S
An Educational Book with Fun Experiments
Fun Science
Experiments
for Kids
Baargavi S
Baargavi S
ORIGIN
OF
UNIVERSE
Universe at your finger tips
My Journal
of
Science
Exploring never ends...
Baargavi S

My journey with birds
BAARGAVI S

SHOULD WE SEARCH FOR ALIENS
Written by Baargavi S

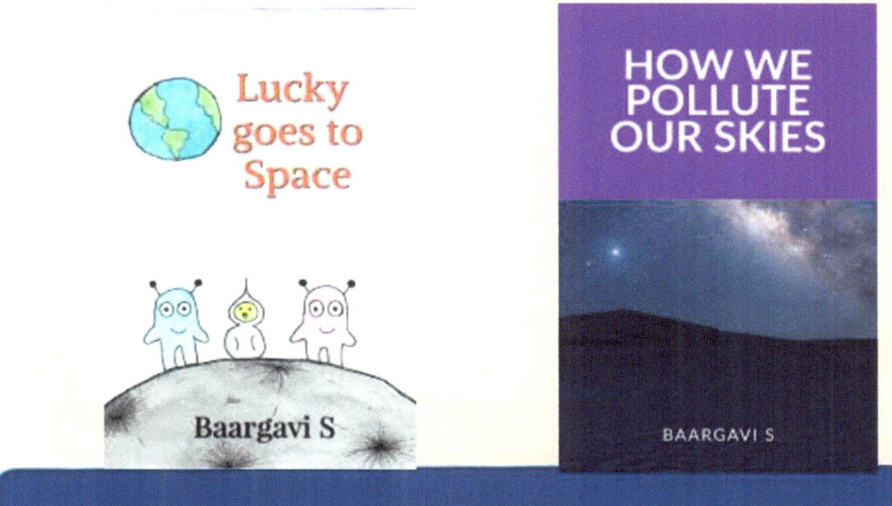

Lucky goes to Space
Baargavi S
HOW WE POLLUTE OUR SKIES
BAARGAVI S

With this, we have reached the end of the Galactic Gallery. Thank you so much for visiting our gallery!

We hope you enjoyed your visit. Do visit us again. Good bye dear visitor!